# SCORPIONS!

## STRANGE AND WONDERFUL

Laurence Pringle

Illustrated by Meryl Henderson

BOYDS MILLS PRESS
AN IMPRINT OF HIGHLIGHTS

*In memory of "scorpion man" Gary A. Polis,*
*a great scientist, husband, father, friend.*
*—LP*

*To Janice and Joe Lukas.*
*I treasure our long and happy friendship.*
*—MH*

The author thanks Dr. Victor Fet, Department of Biological Sciences, Marshall University, for his thorough review of the text and illustrations.

Text copyright © 2013 by Laurence Pringle
Illustrations copyright © 2013 by Meryl Henderson
All rights reserved
*For information about permission to reproduce selections from this book, please contact permissions@highlights.com.*

Boyds Mills Press, Inc.
An Imprint of Highlights
815 Church Street
Honesdale, Pennsylvania 18431
Printed in China

ISBN: 978-1-59078-473-0
Library of Congress Control Number: 2013931088

First edition
The text of this book is set in Goudy Oldstyle.

10 9 8 7 6 5 4 3 2 1

## It is twilight in the desert.

A lizard scampers along, hurrying to a safe hideout among the rocks. Suddenly it is grabbed by a scorpion's powerful claws. The lizard struggles. It tries to break free, but the scorpion's poisonous stinger flashes through the air. It stabs the lizard again and again, injecting venom into the lizard's body.

Soon the lizard lies still. The scorpion begins to feast on its prey.

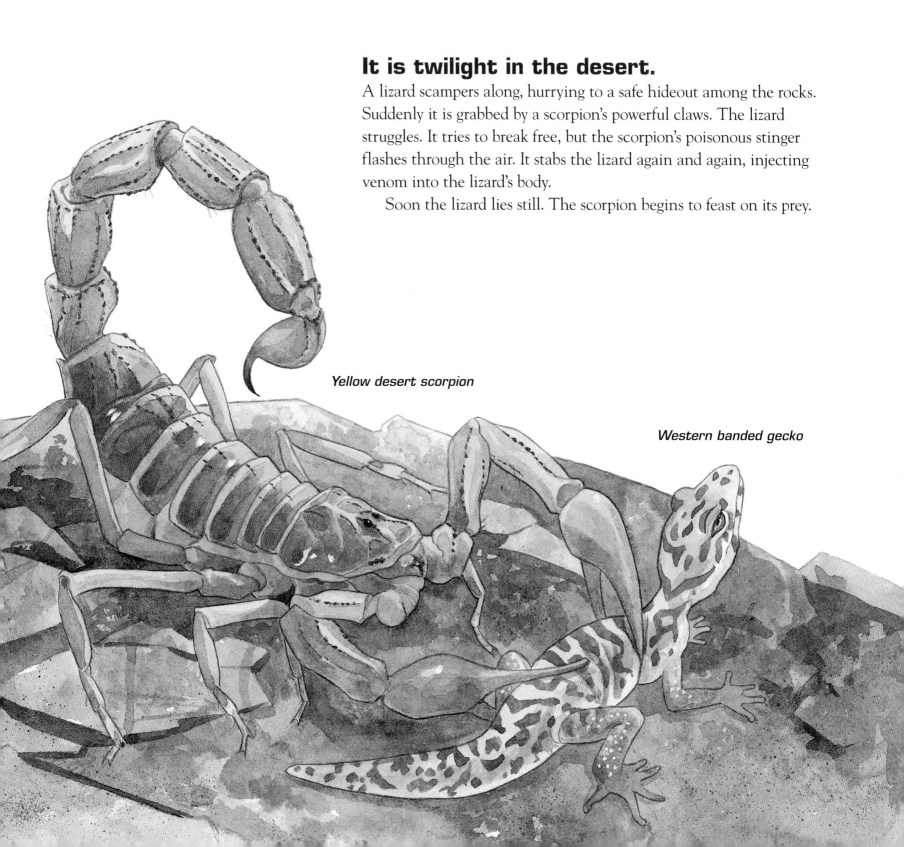

*Yellow desert scorpion*

*Western banded gecko*

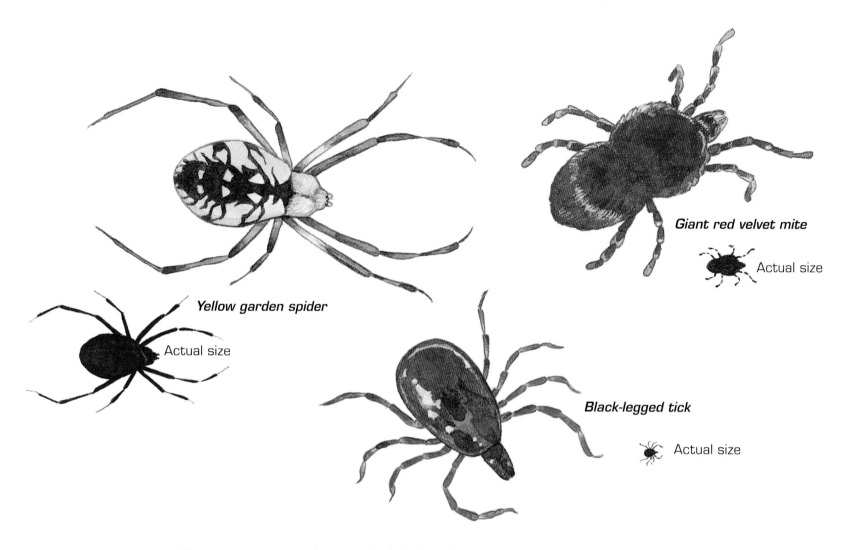

**Yellow garden spider**

Actual size

**Giant red velvet mite**

Actual size

**Black-legged tick**

Actual size

All scorpions are predators, which kill and eat other living things. All scorpions have poisonous stingers that they can use to kill prey and to defend themselves. All scorpions have the same basic body shape.

However, scientists who study scorpions rarely say "all scorpions" because scorpions differ so much. They vary a lot in size, in behavior, and in the places they live. So this book reveals not just facts about all scorpions, but also about the amazing variety of these scary but fascinating creatures.

Scorpions are arachnids (uh-RACK-nids). Arachnids include spiders, ticks, and mites. All arachnids have eight legs (insects have six). Some creatures have the word "scorpion" in their names—water scorpions, wind scorpions, false scorpions, whip scorpions—but none of them are true scorpions!

**Water scorpion**
Actual size

**False scorpion**
Actual size

**Giant whip scorpion**
Actual size

**Pale wind scorpion**
Actual size

Water scorpions live underwater in ponds and slow-flowing streams. Their strong front legs look somewhat like the pinching claws of scorpions, but water scorpions are insects, not arachnids.

Wind scorpions run fast, "like the wind." These arachnids have big, pincer-like claws, but have no poison glands. All true scorpions have poison glands.

False scorpions (also called pseudoscorpions) are tiny arachnids. Most are less than one-fifth of an inch (five millimeters) long. They have poison glands in their pinching claws, but no tail stinger, as scorpions do.

Most whip scorpions have a long, whip-like tail, but no poisonous stinger. True scorpions have a poisonous stinger. A whip scorpion species that lives in the southern United States can squirt an irritating liquid to repel a bird or other predator. The spray smells like vinegar, so this whip scorpion has an unusual name: vinegaroon.

5

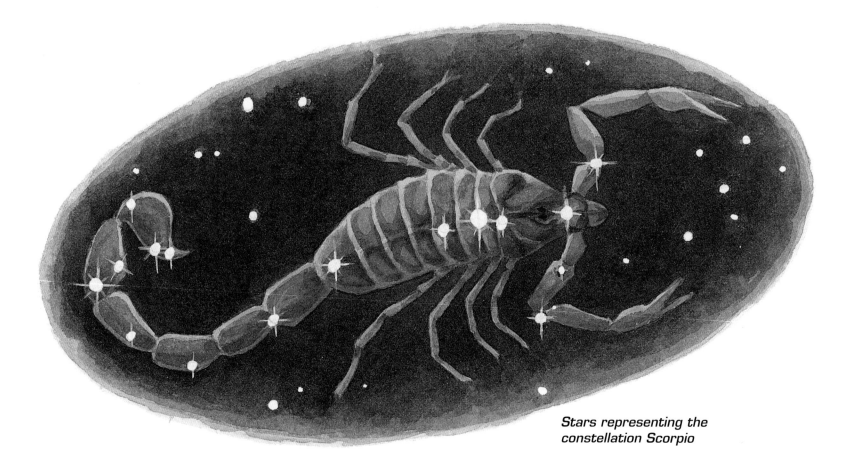

*Stars representing the constellation Scorpio*

Because scorpions can sting, and some can actually kill humans, people long ago made the scorpion a symbol of evil and death. This was true in many cultures. About three thousand years ago, Persians believed that scorpions were sent by an evil spirit to destroy all life. A deadly scorpion also plays a part in ancient Greek legends. A great hunter, Orion, boasted that he could kill any animal on Earth. To protect all living things, Gaia, Mother Earth, sent a giant scorpion to kill Orion. Or, in another tale, the scorpion was sent by the god Apollo.

Later, according to Greek tales, the scorpion was raised into the sky as a constellation called Scorpio. It is a curving sweep of stars near the center of the Milky Way galaxy. Two of the brightest stars, close together, represent Scorpio's stinger. Orion is also a constellation. As the legend tells, Orion and Scorpio were placed as far apart as possible.

When Scorpio appears in the eastern night sky, Orion drops below the western horizon. The scorpion chases the hunter across the sky but never catches him.

*Ancient coin from Pakistan*

*Serket*

In South America, the Mayan name for the constellation of Scorpio means "sign of the death god." Ancient Egyptians believed in a scorpion goddess named Serket (or Selquet or several other spellings), who is shown in art and statues with a scorpion on top of her head. She was believed to have power over all poisonous creatures. According to legend, she protected two rulers, so they were called scorpion kings.

Throughout history and in many cultures, the scorpion image has been used as a symbol of power and evil. That continues to this day. Need a scary, villainous animal for a science-fiction film or video game? Bring in a giant scorpion!

This book is about real, not imaginary, scorpions.

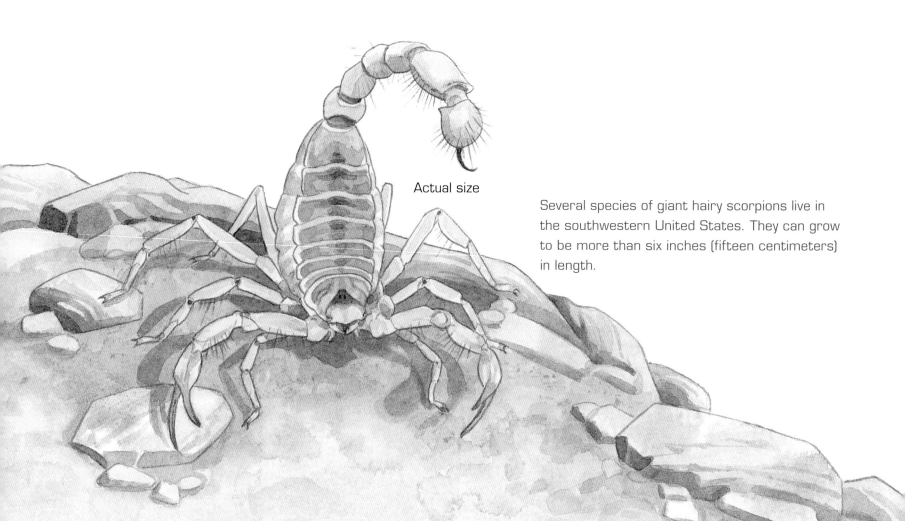

Actual size

Several species of giant hairy scorpions live in the southwestern United States. They can grow to be more than six inches (fifteen centimeters) in length.

Our planet is home to almost two thousand different kinds of scorpions. Biologists expect to discover other species, perhaps several hundred more. They search wherever scorpions might live. They look in deserts, but also in many other wild habitats. Scorpions live in tropical forests, grasslands, along seashores, in caves, and high on mountains. They have been found under snow-covered rocks in Asia's Himalayas and South America's Andes, up to 16,500 feet (5,500 meters) above sea level.

One hundred scorpion species live in the United States. A few are shown here, life size. Their length is measured from mouth to stinger tip.

Northern scorpions are about two inches (five centimeters) long. They live in Nevada and northward, even in southern Alberta and British Columbia, Canada.

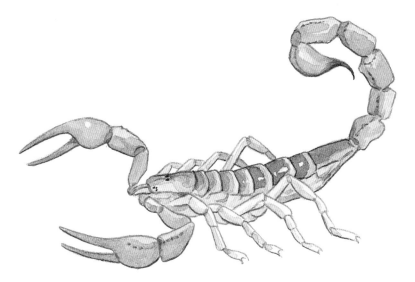

Actual size

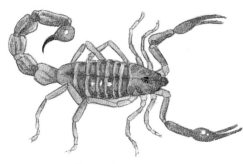

Actual size

Bark scorpions form a group of several species. They often hide under loose tree bark. One dark brown bark species, nearly three inches (about seven centimeters) long, lives in Florida.

Devil scorpions is the name given to another group of several species. They are two to three inches (five to seven centimeters) long. Most live in the southwest. One lives in some southeastern states, including South Carolina.

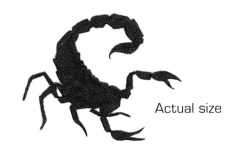

Actual size

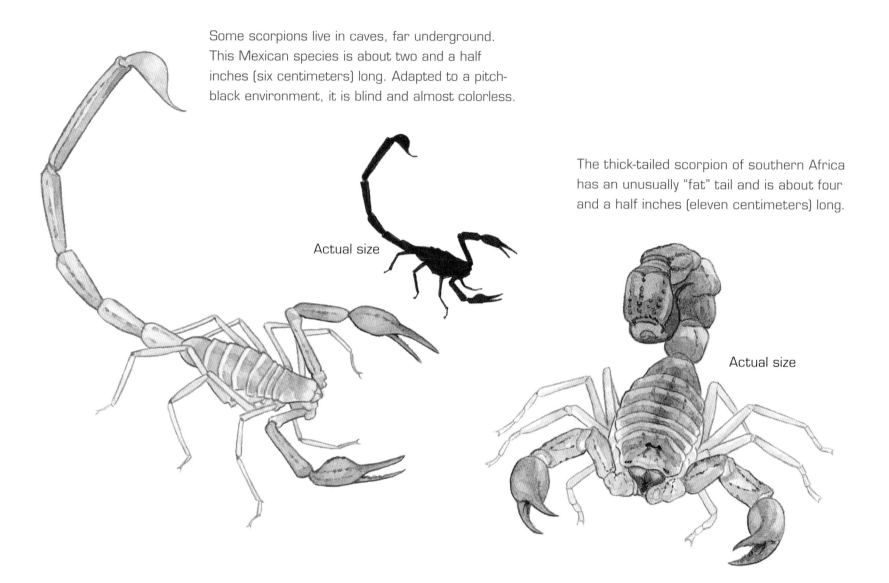

Some scorpions live in caves, far underground. This Mexican species is about two and a half inches (six centimeters) long. Adapted to a pitch-black environment, it is blind and almost colorless.

Actual size

The thick-tailed scorpion of southern Africa has an unusually "fat" tail and is about four and a half inches (eleven centimeters) long.

Actual size

Scorpions are most abundant in warm climates, but live almost worldwide. (There are none in the Arctic or Antarctic.) Their populations are adapted to blend into the colors of different habitats. Species that live in deserts and other dry habitats are usually light brown or yellowish in color. Those that live in forest or mountain habitats that get more rain are usually dark brown or black. As habitats vary, populations of a single species may be pale in one area, dark in another.

Here are some more of Earth's diverse scorpions.

One of the smallest scorpions lives in central Mexico. It measures about a half inch (1.2 centimeters) long. Other very small species live on some Caribbean islands and in the Middle East.

Actual size

The imperial or emperor scorpion, up to eight inches (twenty centimeters) long from mouth to stinger tip, is one of the biggest of all. It lives in tropical western Africa.

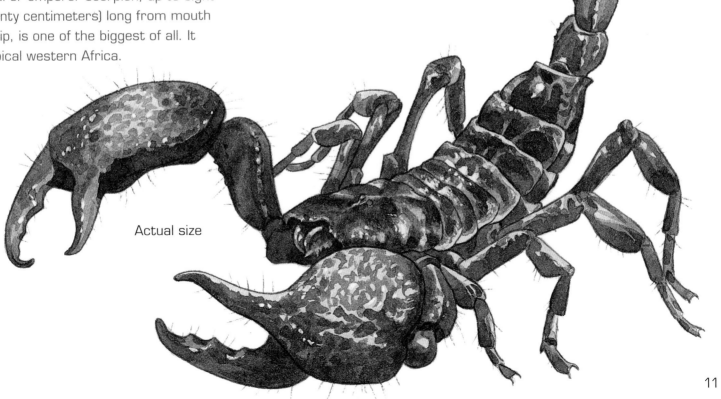

Actual size

Scientists have discovered fossils of extinct creatures that are sometimes called sea scorpions. However, these animals were not closely related to scorpions. They are called eurypterids. Some grew to be more than eight feet (two and a half meters) long. They were the biggest arthropods that ever lived.

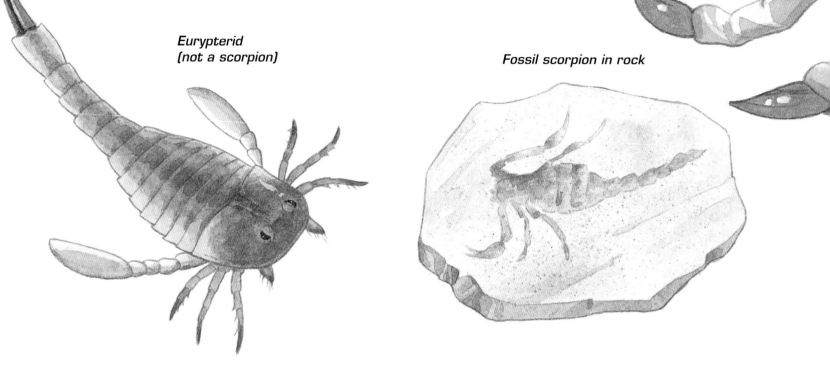

**Eurypterid
(not a scorpion)**

**Fossil scorpion in rock**

Overall, scorpions are big creatures. An average-sized scorpion is bigger than nearly all other arachnids and insects. The largest scorpions are bigger than most lizards, frogs, and mice, rats, and other rodents. Nevertheless, today's scorpions are tiny compared with their ancient ancestors.

Fossils of water-dwelling scorpions have been found in 400-million-year-old rocks. Some measure three feet (one meter) long. Scorpions were among the very first animals to leave water and live on land.

Today's scorpions are smaller, but they have an amazing history: 325 million years of life on land. Scorpions lived before dinosaurs. They lived during the time of dinosaurs. Some were probably hunted and eaten by dinosaurs! The dinosaurs died out, and scorpions lived on. They continue to thrive.

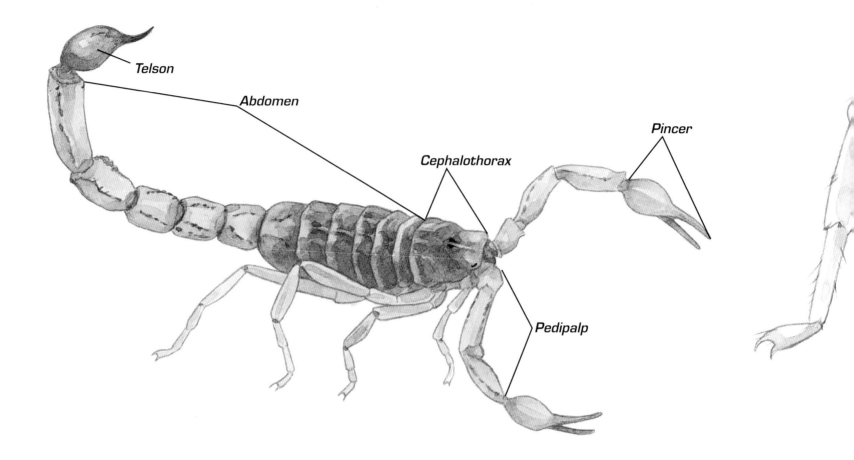

Telson

Abdomen

Cephalothorax

Pincer

Pedipalp

Scorpions today look remarkably like their ancient ancestors. Their basic body plan, their behavior, and their senses continue to make them very successful animals.

Scorpions have no skeleton within their bodies. Instead they have a tough outer exoskeleton made of cuticle. Every scorpion's body has two major parts. Its front, called the cephalothorax, is both its head and body. Its rear part is called the abdomen. The last five segments of the abdomen are narrow, forming a tail. At the tip of the tail is the telson. It contains two glands that produce poison, and ends with a curved stinger. Tiny ducts carry poison from the glands to openings near the stinger's tip.

A scorpion walks on four pairs of legs, each tipped with tiny claws. In front of these are pedipalps—clawed arms with pincers at the ends. They grab and hold prey, and help dig burrows. The scorpion's mouth is also armed with small pincers that tear up food and push it into its mouth.

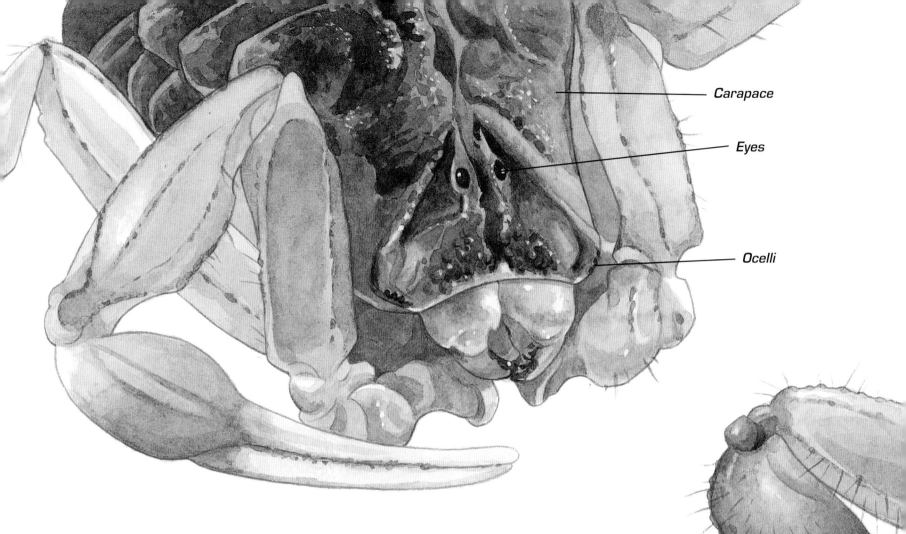

Carapace

Eyes

Ocelli

Stinger

The top of the cephalothorax is covered by a tough shield called the carapace. Two eyes peer out from the front center of the carapace. Also, at the front corners of the carapace are two clusters of tiny eyes, called ocelli.

Despite all of their eyes, scorpions do not see very well. Keen eyesight is not vital because scorpions have other senses that help them catch food and avoid enemies. Their eyes are special in one way: they are highly sensitive to low levels of light. To scorpions, moonlight may be as bright as sunlight is to humans. When the moon is full, desert scorpions usually hide in their shelters.

Male    Female

Flat rock scorpion

Although all scorpions have the same basic body plan, some differ quite a bit from others. For example, female scorpions are bigger than males, sometimes almost double their size. (In a few species, the opposite is true, with bigger males.)

Some scorpion species can live in a variety of habitats, while others are more specialized. This specialization affects how they live and how they look. Scorpions that live mostly in rocky areas need to slip easily under stones and into narrow crevices. They have flat, long bodies and pedipalps.

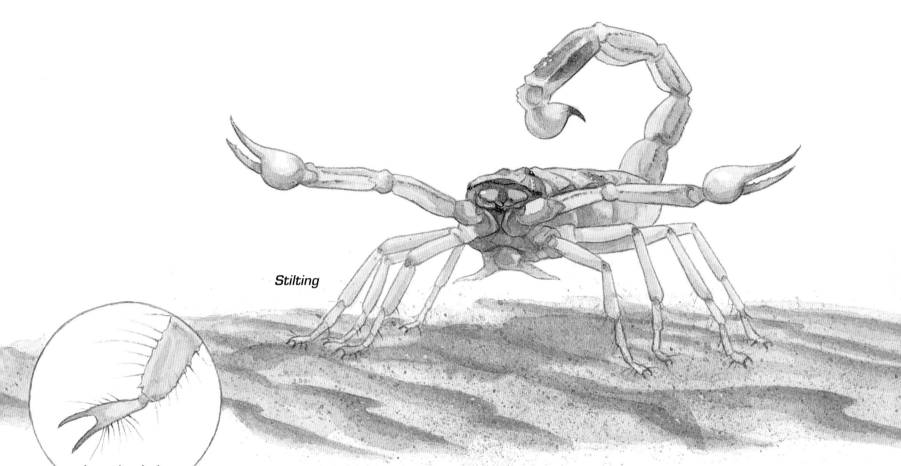

Stilting

Long leg hairs

Scorpions that live in desert areas sometimes need to move swiftly on loose sand. Their legs are adapted in two ways to do this. They have extra-long claws on the ends of their legs and long hairs that stick out from their legs. These adaptations spread their weight over the surface and help keep them from sinking into sand.

A desert-dwelling scorpion also can move or stand in an unusual way that helps it survive. Sunlit sand can be fiercely hot, as much as 140 degrees Fahrenheit (60 degrees Celsius). Usually, a scorpion rests in a hideout during the hottest time of day. If necessary, however, it can stay on hot sand by "stilting"—standing tall on its legs, keeping its body away from the surface.

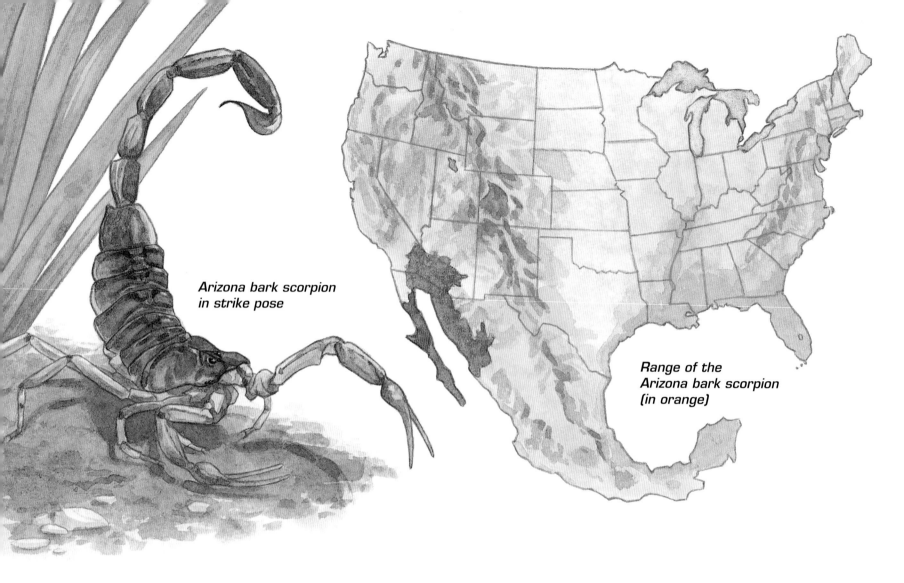

*Arizona bark scorpion in strike pose*

*Range of the Arizona bark scorpion (in orange)*

When people look at a scorpion, or just think about one, they usually focus on one part: the poisonous stinger. It is in plain sight, right on the tip of the tail. Although the stinger is sharp and can be deadly, humans do not usually die from scorpion stings.

Scorpion poison can kill a cricket, lizard, or mouse, but the sting of only about three dozen species—out of almost 2,000—can kill a person. Just one of these dangerous species, the Arizona bark scorpion, lives in the United States. It's found in the southwest, mostly in Arizona. It's also found in neighboring Mexico, home to a number of other kinds of scorpions that are a threat to people. The other deadliest species live in warm tropical climates: the Middle East, Africa, and South America.

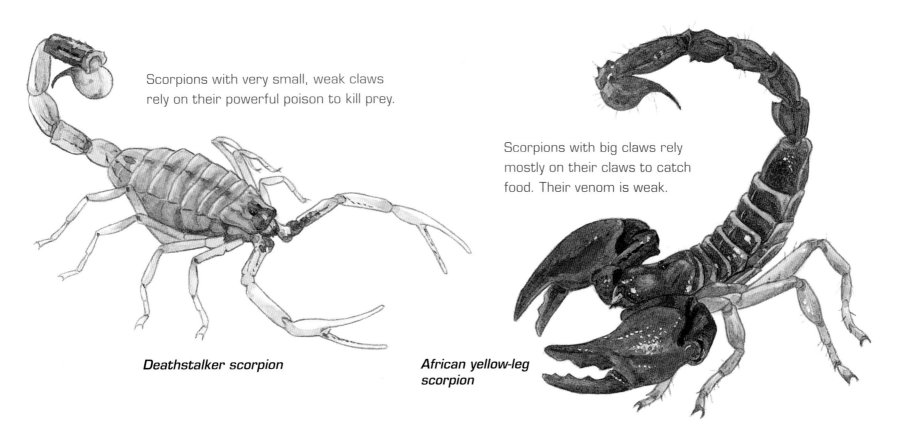

Scorpions with very small, weak claws rely on their powerful poison to kill prey.

Scorpions with big claws rely mostly on their claws to catch food. Their venom is weak.

**Deathstalker scorpion**

**African yellow-leg scorpion**

Scorpion venom contains neurotoxins—chemicals that affect a victim's nervous system. These chemicals can stop a person's breathing or cause heart failure. Medicines called antivenins defeat the neurotoxins and save lives. Wherever the most deadly scorpions live, hospitals and clinics keep supplies of antivenins.

Nevertheless, the few species truly dangerous to people take quite a toll. Each year several thousand people, mostly children, die from scorpion stings. Small children are most vulnerable. They often play outdoors in the tropics, and may accidentally disturb a scorpion. Also, a dose of venom is more concentrated, and more life-threatening, in a small child than in a bigger person.

The sting of nearly all scorpion species is often no more painful than a bee or wasp sting. And all scorpions flee or hide from people. They sting only to defend themselves (or to kill prey). Although it is wise never to touch any scorpion, it is also helpful to be able to tell a rather harmless kind from a deadly species.

Look at the scorpions on this page. One is especially scary looking, with its massive pedipalps and pincers. The other has thin, tiny pedipalps and pincers. Which scorpion has the most dangerous venom in its stinger? (The answer is in the labels by the scorpions.)

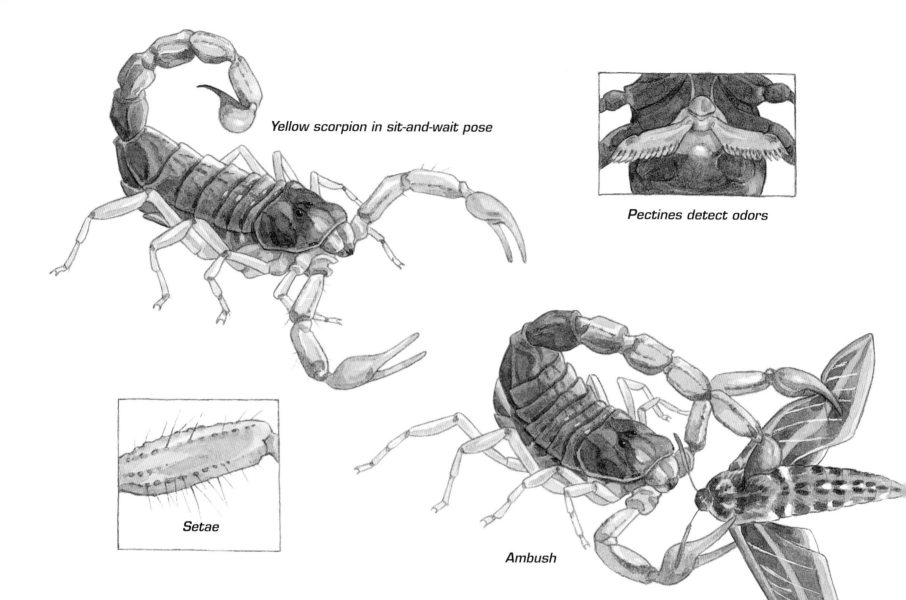

Yellow scorpion in sit-and-wait pose

Pectines detect odors

Setae

Ambush

Some kinds of scorpions move about, hunting for food. One Australian species creeps into the burrows of spiders to catch them. However, most scorpion species are sit-and-wait predators. When darkness falls they leave their hideouts, then wait to ambush an insect or other prey animal that comes near.

On their bodies and legs, scorpions have hairs (called setae) that are highly sensitive to touch. Other kinds of smaller sensitive hairs on their pedipalps can sense disturbances in the air caused by a moth or other flying insect. Even with weak eyesight, scorpions can detect and snatch insects from the air.

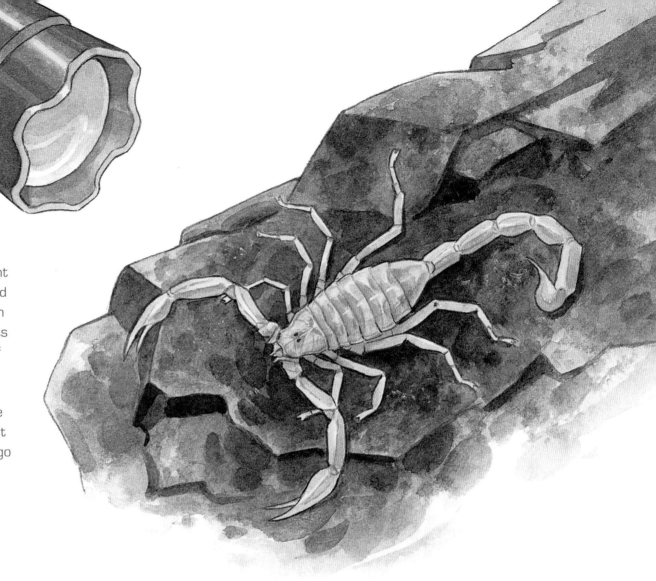

Studying wild scorpions at night was once a challenge. They fled when a flashlight was shone on them. Then, in 1954, scientists learned that scorpions give off a bluish glow under ultraviolet light (also called UV or "black" light). This light does not scare scorpions. Biologists can use it to observe scorpions as they go about their normal lives in the night.

The legs of scorpions also have sensory cells—on their leg tips, on hairs, and in slits in the legs. These make it possible for scorpions to feel vibrations made by an insect or other prey animal walking as far as three feet (one meter) away. Finally, scorpions have other sense organs, called pectines, on the underside of their abdomens. Pectines can detect odors on the surface—from prey or from a possible mate.

Once an insect or other prey is detected, a scorpion rushes toward it and seizes it with its pedipalps. A big animal, struggling to escape, is stung with venom. Smaller animals are crushed by pincers or simply held tightly and eaten alive.

*Asian forest scorpion*

A scorpion eats slowly. It doesn't chew and swallow. It first tears an insect or other prey apart, beginning with its head. The scorpion also lets out fluids that begin to digest the food. Digestion starts outside the mouth, as bits of food dissolve into a soup that is then pumped into the mouth and swallowed.

Usually a scorpion needs several hours to finish a meal. Then it may not eat again for several weeks or longer. Since scorpions do not travel far (except during mating season) and since they usually sit and wait for prey, they use very little energy. Scorpions have an amazing ability to go a long time without food, up to a year in some desert species. (Scorpions also get along with very little water. The water that is part of the bodies of their prey may be all they need.)

A hungry scorpion is not very choosy. Any creature on the move, of the right size, can be dinner. For big scorpions this can be a lizard, mouse, or snake. Scorpions also eat centipedes, millipedes, beetles, flies, moths, butterflies, worms, and spiders (including tarantulas).

Indian ornamental
black and white tarantula

Asian forest scorpion

23

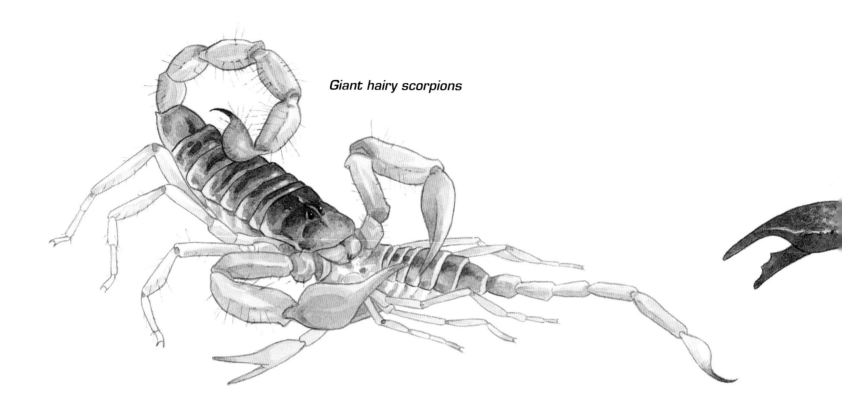

*Giant hairy scorpions*

One of the most common foods of many scorpions is—other scorpions! A scorpion usually attacks prey smaller than itself. That is the key factor, not whether the prey is an insect or a scorpion. Also, when a scorpion grabs a smaller scorpion to eat, it cannot tell if its prey is from another species or is its own brother.

Sometimes up to half of a scorpion's diet is other scorpions, often including members of its own species. (Animals that eat others of their own species are called cannibals.) Scorpion-on-scorpion predation can have a big effect on the size of a scorpion population. When biologists removed several thousand big scorpions from an area of California desert, the populations of two smaller species grew. One increased six times in abundance.

When giant hairy scorpions are young, they are small enough to be eaten by adult sand scorpions. Eventually, those that survive become the biggest scorpions. Then they eat lots of sand scorpions. You might call this "Revenge of the Giant Hairy Scorpions!"

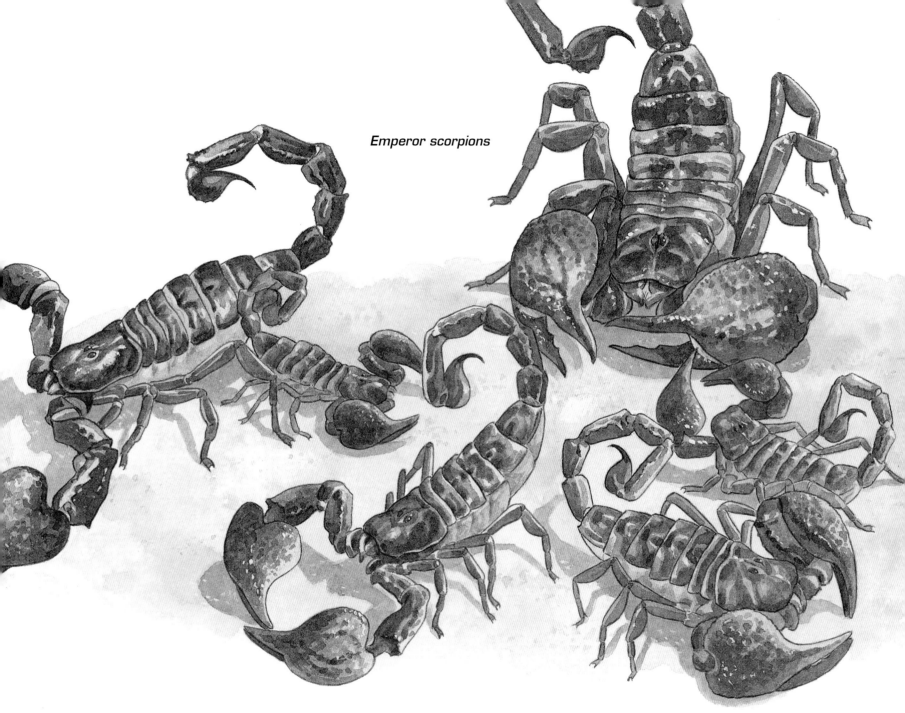

*Emperor scorpions*

Most scorpions are loners, but some gather in groups. In wintertime, a dozen or more scorpions may cluster together in a sheltered place. And in Africa, families of emperor scorpions live together peacefully. The adults catch mice, frogs, and other food, then chew and start to digest it for their young to eat.

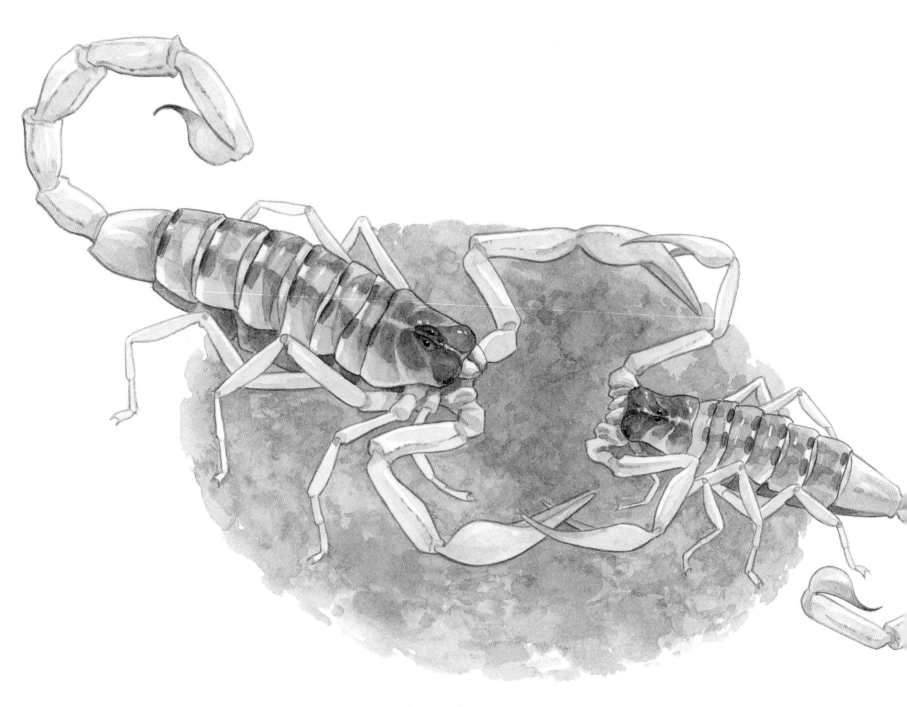

*A sometimes-deadly dance*

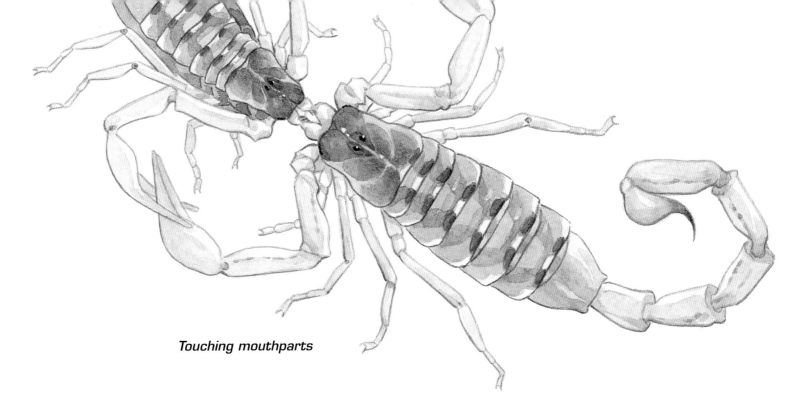

*Touching mouthparts*

During human courtship and dating, people often go dancing. Courting scorpions also do a kind of dance. There is no music, of course, and the evening may end with the death of one of the dancers.

In the mating season, male scorpions roam about, seeking a mate. (This is generally true. Scorpions vary a lot, and in some species females search for males.) A male finds a female of his species by detecting her scent in the air. He grasps her claws with his, then leads her in dance-like motions, sideways, backward, forward—sometimes for a few minutes, sometimes for hours. In some species, the pair touch their mouthparts together in a kind of kiss. Also, early in the dance the male may sting his partner. This does no harm and seems to make her less aggressive.

Dancing around, the male is actually searching for a pebble, stick, or other hard object on the surface. On it he releases a sticky spermatophore. It contains a pack of male sex cells. Then he steers his partner so that she is right over the spermatophore, and those cells can be taken into her body. The mating dance ends.

Once this happens, the male is likely to give his mate a hard smack with his tail and run away. You can probably guess why. Since males are usually smaller than females, they can become an after-dance meal for their partners.

27

*Mother scorpion with young*

Scorpions are remarkable in many ways, but especially in their reproduction. Young scorpions develop within their mother's body for a very long time. This span of time, called the gestation period, ranges from about two months to two years. This means that some scorpions have a gestation time longer than that of people (nine months) or of sperm whales (sixteen months). Overall, baby scorpions take longer to develop than cats, dogs, cows, and most other mammals.

Scorpions are born alive. They do not hatch from eggs (though some kinds need to break free from a thin surrounding membrane). Nearly all other arachnids, including spiders, hatch from eggs. So do insects. Being born alive makes scorpion reproduction more like that of mammals.

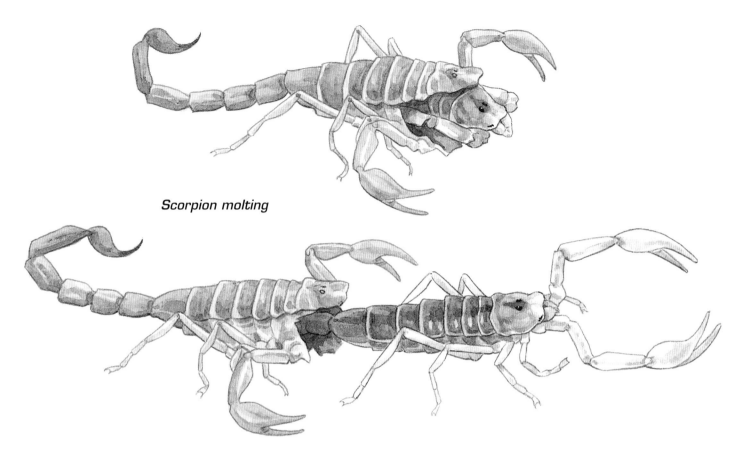

*Scorpion molting*

Scorpion mothers can give birth to as many as one hundred young, though the average is about twenty-five. Immediately after being born, each little scorpion scrambles up one of mom's legs and settles onto her back. In some species the young are scattered about on her back; in others they line up in neat rows. If one falls off, mom picks it up and sets it back on top. (She knows her young by their scent.)

At first, baby scorpions are white. Relying on food stored in their bodies, they do not need to eat. They take in water that passes through their mother's back and through their thin, soft cuticle. Soon their safe piggyback ride on mom comes to an end. Within a week or two, each young has its first molt. Its cuticle splits open, and the little scorpion emerges in a roomier, darker body.

The young scorpions leap from their mother's back and scatter, ready to hunt on their own. They may never be near their mother again. That is a good thing. You can guess what might happen if one of her young came near her hideout when she was hungry.

After molting about five to eight times, a scorpion reaches full adult size. (If it has lost a leg, a replacement may gradually grow back, matching the other legs after a few molts.) Growing to be an adult can take between six months and several years. Although some scorpion species can live for twenty-five years, most survive for just a few.

Many never live to adulthood because they are eaten by predators—and not just bigger scorpions. In daytime, certain kinds of lizards and snakes hunt for scorpions. Birds called roadrunners in the southwestern United States eat many scorpions. At night, owls and bats swoop down to catch them. Centipedes and spiders, including tarantulas, also hunt scorpions at night.

Some predators seem immune to scorpions' venom. Also, owls and several other kinds of predators protect themselves by breaking off a scorpion's tail (with its stinger) before eating the rest or feeding it to their young. Worldwide, these predators include baboons, mongooses, and meerkats.

As prey and as predators, scorpions are part of many food webs. They play major roles in the ecology of deserts and of other habitats where they are plentiful. They are important in other ways, too. Medical scientists have found that scorpion venom can be used to stop damage from strokes (sudden attacks that can leave people paralyzed). Also, an ingredient in scorpion venom helps detect cancer cells. Scientists expect to find other ways in which knowledge about scorpions will help humans.

Real scorpions are not at all like the evil-doers of long-ago myths. They are fascinating creatures, vital in their natural habitats, and full of secrets yet to be discovered.

*Barn owl attacking a giant hairy scorpion*

## To Learn More

### Books and Periodicals

Billings, Charlene W. *Scorpions*. New York: Dodd, Mead & Co., 1983.

Brodie, Edmund D. *Venomous Animals*. New York: Golden Press, 1989.

Polis, Gary. "Why I Love Scorpions." *Boys' Life*, August 1992, 10–13.

Pringle, Laurence. *Scorpion Man: Exploring the World of Scorpions*. New York: Atheneum, 1994.

Richardson, Adele. *Scorpions*. Mankato, MN: Capstone Press, 2003.

Ross, John. "In the Company of Cannibals that Sting . . . and Glow." *Smithsonian Magazine*, April 1996, 92–103.

Rubio, Manny. *Scorpions: Everything about Purchase, Care, Feeding, and Housing*. Hauppauge, NY: Barrons Educational Series, 2008.

Stockmann, Roland, and Ythier, Eric. *Scorpions of the World*. Verrières-le-Buisson, France: NAP Editions, 2010.

### Websites*

Arizona Scorpions
Arizona Cooperative Extension
University of Arizona College of Agriculture and Life Sciences
ag.arizona.edu/pubs/insects/az1223

Arizona-Sonora Desert Museum
desertmuseum.org/books/nhsd_scorpions_new.php

Texas Scorpions
AgriLife Extension Service
Texas A&M University College of Agriculture and Life Sciences
insects.tamu.edu/extension/publications/epubs/e_362.cfm

### Sources

Information sources for this book include the previously listed books, periodicals, and websites, but especially the following:
Polis, Gary A. *The Biology of Scorpions*. Stanford, CA: Stanford University Press, 1990.

This book remains the most comprehensive source of information on the subject. In nearly 600 pages and twelve chapters, ten experts report on scorpion anatomy, biogeography, life history, behavior, ecology, mythology, and the chemistry and effects of scorpion venom.

## Pronunciation Guide

| | |
|---|---|
| **antivenin** | an-tee-VEN-in |
| **arachnid** | uh-RACK-nid |
| **arthropod** | AR-thruh-pod |
| **carapace** | CARE-uh-pace |
| **cephalothorax** | sef-uh-la-THOR-acks |
| **cuticle** | QUE-te-cull |
| **eurypterid** | yuh-RIP-tuh-rid |
| **gestation** | jess-TAY-shun |
| **neurotoxins** | NUR-oh-tock-sins |
| **ocelli** | oh-SELL-eye |
| **pectines** | PECK-te-nez |
| **pedipalp** | PED-uh-palp |
| **setae** | SEE-tee |
| **spermatophore** | spur-MAT-uh-for |